Perfume Pagoda Festival

T0362855

Beautiful Cave

We are going

to the Perfume Pagoda.

We are going in a boat.

We will row

and row

and row.

On the way

we will see our friends.

On the way

we will see **water lilies**.

On the way

we will see **rice paddies**.

On the way

we will see temples.

13

Here we are

at the Perfume Pagoda.

15

Glossary

rice paddies

water lilies